REVISED EDITION

The Complete Lord's Prayer for Every Busy Accompanist

By
Albert Hay Malotte

ISBN 978-0-7935-5321-1

G. SCHIRMER, Inc.

DISTRIBUTED BY

HAL•LEONARD®
CORPORATION
7777 W. BLUEMOUND RD. P.O. BOX 13819 MILWAUKEE, WI 53213

Visit us online
www.schirmer.com
www.halleonard.com

The Complete Lord's Prayer for Every Busy Accompanist

Gratefully dedicated to my friend John Charles Thomas

The Lord's Prayer

Albert Hay Malotte

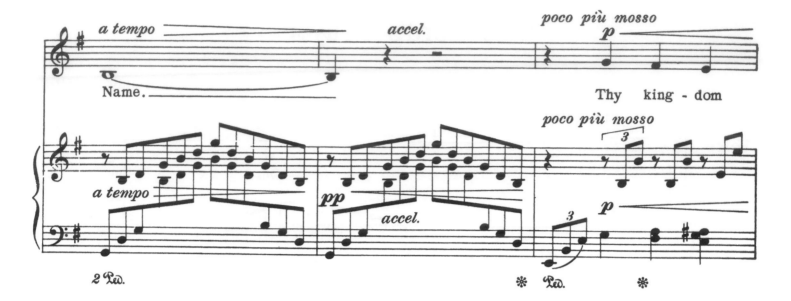

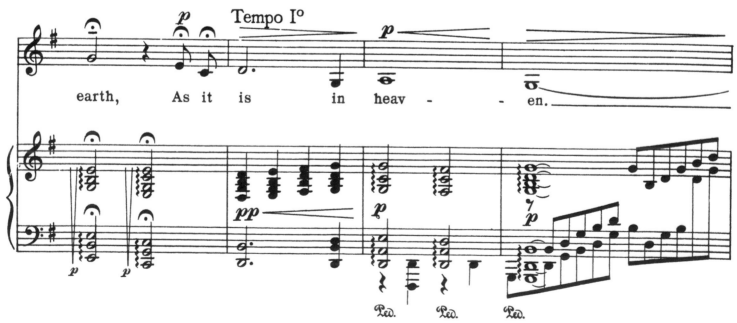

L'istesso tempo

pp molto espressivo e sempre legato

Give us this day our

dai - ly bread. And for-give us our debts,_____ As
tres-pass-es As

poco accel.

8

pow - er, _____ and the glo - - - ry, _____ for

ev - - - er. _____ A - - -
and ev - - er. A -

men. _____
men. _____

ral - len - tan - do e morendo

Gratefully dedicated to my friend John Charles Thomas

The Lord's Prayer

Albert Hay Malotte

L'istesso tempo

Give us this day our

dai - ly bread. And for-give us our debts,___ As
tres-pass-es As

Gratefully dedicated to my friend John Charles Thomas

The Lord's Prayer

Albert Hay Malotte

L'istesso tempo

Gratefully dedicated to my friend John Charles Thomas

The Lord's Prayer

Albert Hay Malotte

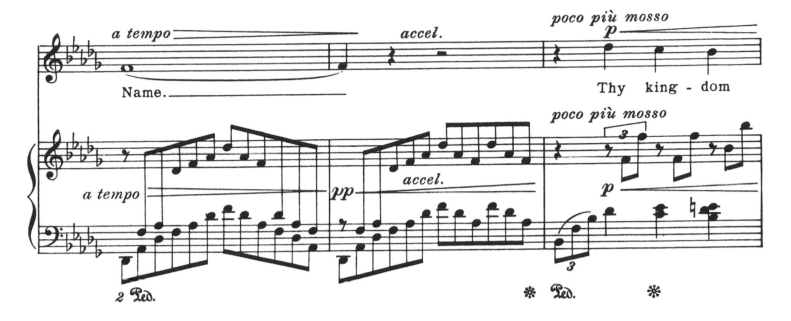

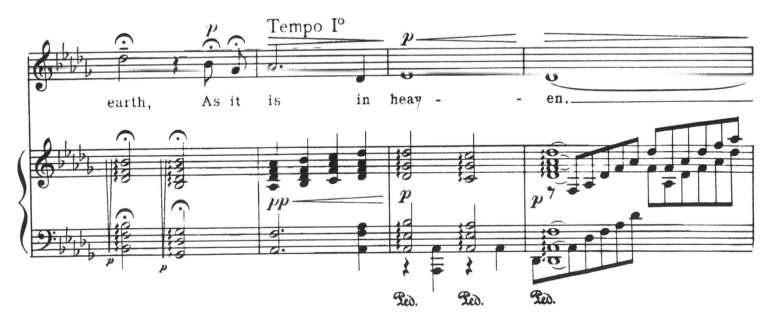

L'istesso tempo

23

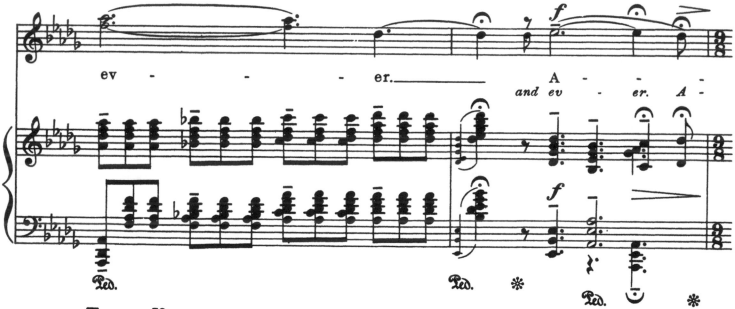

Gratefully dedicated to my friend John Charles Thomas

The Lord's Prayer

Albert Hay Malotte

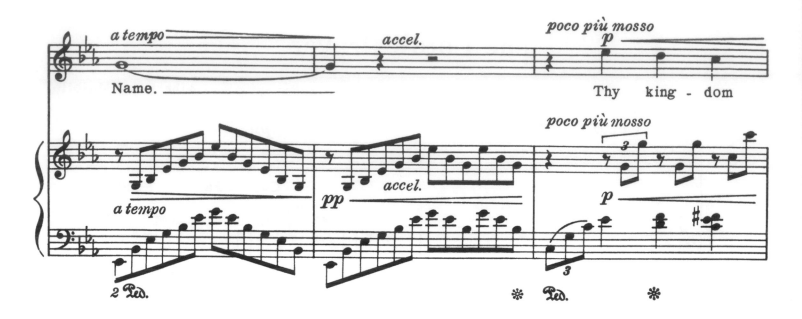

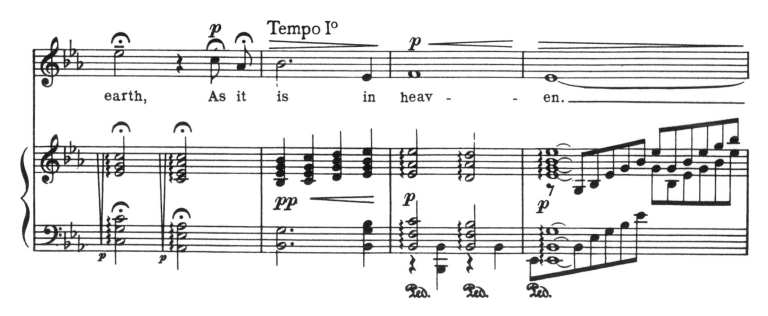

L'istesso tempo

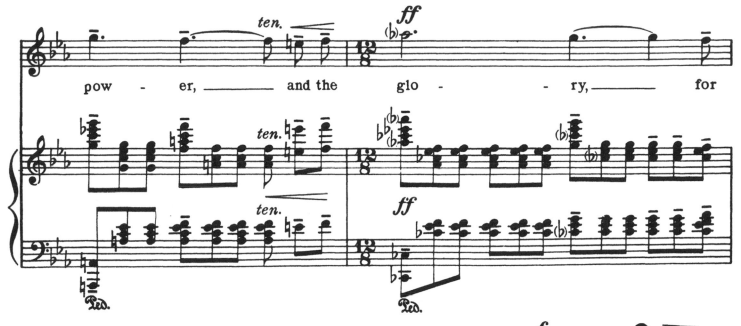

pow - er, _____ and the glo - ry, _____ for

ev - - - er. _____ A - -

and ev - er. A -

Tempo I°

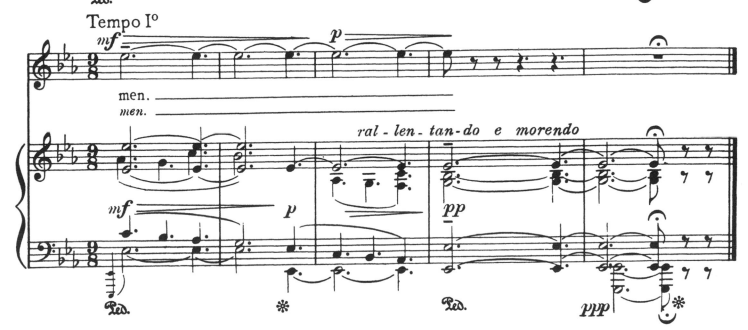

men. _____

men. _____

ral - len - tan - do e morendo

The Lord's Prayer

Great *mf*
Swell *pp* to Great
Choir soft 8′ 4′
Pedal soft 16′ 8′

Albert Hay Malotte
Organ Accompaniment
arranged by Carl Weinrich

L'istesso tempo

Give us this day our

dai - ly bread. And for- give us our debts,____ As
tres-pass-es As

33

Poco meno mosso, e sonoramente

34

king - dom,___ and the pow - er,___ and the glo - ry,___ for

ev - - - er._____ and ev - er. A-

Tempo I°

men._____
men._____

ral - len - tan - do e morendo

The Lord's Prayer

Great *mf*
Swell *pp* to Great
Choir soft 8' 4'
Pedal soft 16' 8'

Albert Hay Malotte
Organ Accompaniment
arranged by Carl Weinrich

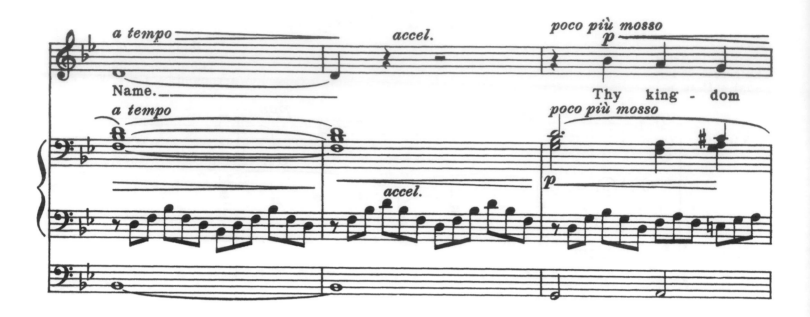

L'istesso tempo

we _____ for-give our debt - ors.
we for-give those who tres-pass a - gainst us.

And lead us not in-to temp-ta - tion; But de-

liv - er us from e - vil: For thine is the

king - dom,___ and the pow - er,___ and the glo - ry,___ for

ev - - - - er.___ A -
and ev - er. A -

men.___
men.___

Tempo I°

ral - len - tan - do   e   morendo

reduce

The Lord's Prayer

Great *mf*
Swell *pp* to Great
Choir soft 8′ 4′
Pedal soft 16′ 8′

Albert Hay Malotte
Organ Accompaniment
arranged by Carl Weinrich

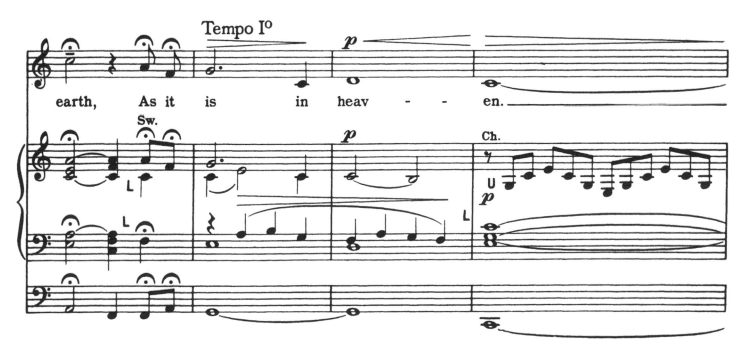

L'istesso tempo

Give us this day our

dai - ly bread. And for-give us our debts, ____ As
tres - pass-es As

king - dom, ____ and the pow - er, ____ and the glo ry, ____ for

ev - - - er. _____ A - -

and ev - er. A -

Tempo I°

men. _____

men. _____

ral - len - tan - do e morendo

reduce

The Lord's Prayer

Albert Hay Malotte
Organ Accompaniment
arranged by Carl Weinrich

Great *mf*
Swell *pp* to Great
Choir soft 8′ 4′
Pedal soft 16′ 8′

36946 c

48

26946

king - dom,___ and the pow - er,___ and the gło - ry,___ for

ev - - - - er._____ A - - -
and ev - er. A -

Tempo I°

men._____
men._____

ral - len - tan - do e morendo

reduce

The Lord's Prayer

Albert Hay Malotte
Organ Accompaniment
arranged by Carl Weinrich

Great *mf*
Swell *pp* to Great
Choir soft 8′ 4′
Pedal soft 16′ 8′

*The Piano Solo (Easy Version) edition of *The Lord's Prayer* or the Piano Duet edition or the Piano and Organ edition may be used in place of this accompaniment.

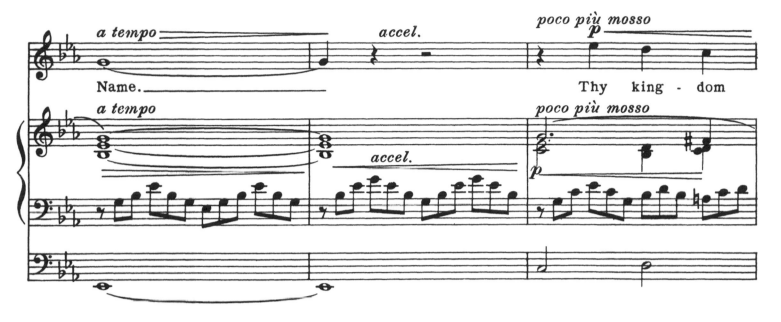

L'istesso tempo

Give us this day our

dai - ly bread. And for-give us our debts, ___ As
tres-pass-es As

54

king - dom,___ and the pow - er,___ and the glo - ry,___ for

ev - - - - - er.___ A - - -
and ev - er. A-

Tempo Iº

men.___
men.___
ral - len - tan - do   e   morendo
reduce

The Lord's Prayer

Transcribed for piano
by Carl Deis
from the original setting for voice and piano

Albert Hay Malotte

Tempo I°

pp molto espressivo e sempre legato

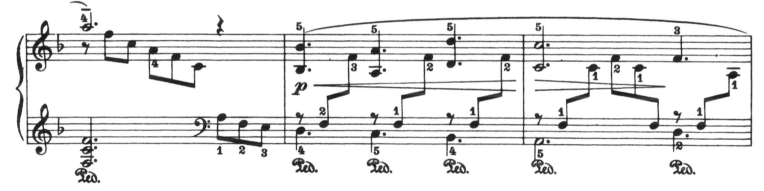

poco accel.

rallentando

pp

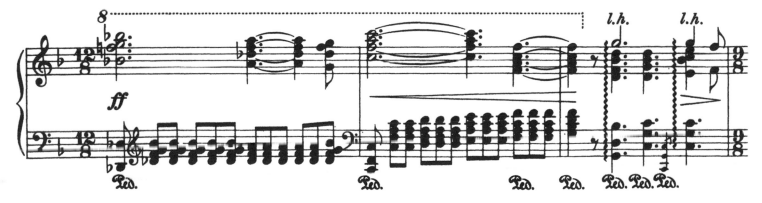

The Lord's Prayer

For a Three Manual Organ:
Sw: Strings 8′, Flutes 8′, prepare
Celeste 8′ on Piston 1
Gt: Strings 8′, Flutes 8′, 4′, Diapason 8′, 4′, +Swell
+ Choir, prepare Chimes on Piston 1
Ch: Clarinet or Diapason
Ped: Bourdon 16′ + Swell

For a Two Manual Organ:
Sw.: Strings 8′, Flute 8′, prepare
Celeste 8′ on Piston 1
Gt.: Diapason 8′ + Swell
Ped.: Bourdon 16′ + Swell

Prepare

U Bb ⑩	00	5885	463
U Bb ⑪	00	8870	000
L Bb ⑩	00	4631	000
P	52		

Albert Hay Malotte
Arranged by Henrietta Dippman Griswold

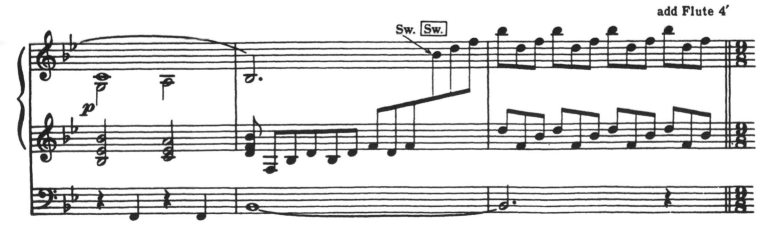

60

open Crescendo Pedal 1/4
LG 7
open Crescendo Pedal 1/2
Poco meno
Gt.
mf
Gt. Gt.
rit.
LG 7
mosso e sonoramente
open Crescendo Pedal full
f
Gt.
ff
f
close Cresc. Pedal
L B♭ 10
off Flute 4′
Sw. Sw.
Sw. Sw. Piston 1
Gt. Piston 1
Geigen off
L
p
rall. e morendo
pp

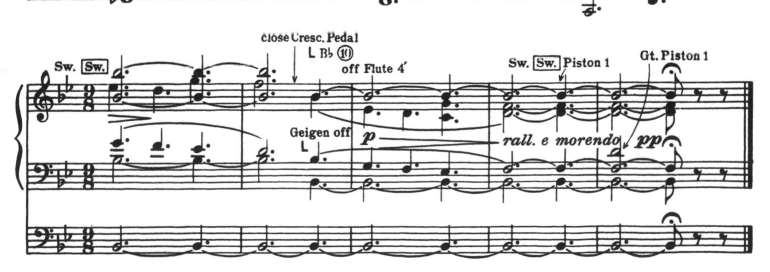

The Lord's Prayer

Albert Hay Malotte
Arranged by Carl Deis

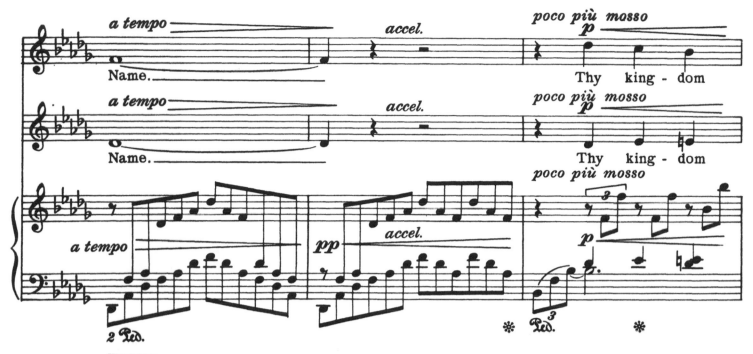

The Lord's Prayer

Albert Hay Malotte
Arranged by Carl Deis

L'istesso tempo

70

*If desired, Soprano and Tenor may exchange parts in this and the succeeding measure.

The Lord's Prayer

Albert Hay Malotte
Arranged by Carl Deis

74

L'istesso tempo